Blessed

A Journey through Grief to Gratitude

Philip L. Winteregg

ISBN 979-8-89345-633-2 (paperback)
ISBN 979-8-89345-634-9 (digital)

Christian Faith Publishing
832 Park Avenue
Meadville, PA 16335
www.christianfaithpublishing.com

Printed in the United States of America

You turned my wailing into dancing;
you removed my sackcloth and clothed me with joy,
that my heart may sing your praises and not be silent.
Lord my God, I will praise you forever.

—Psalm 30:11–12

FOREWORD

Grief is one of the most difficult challenges to navigate. However, it is something that all of us will be required to walk through at some point in our lives, and no two people will walk the same path. The questions that may bombard your mind can feel overwhelming. "Is what I'm feeling normal?" "Is this decision I'm making going to be misconstrued by those looking at my life from the outside?" "How long is too long before I do this, or was it long enough?" "Is there a certain length of time for each stage of grief?" See how exhausting this can be?

Phil has written an incredible testimonial about his navigation through grief. In his book, *Blessed: A Journey through Grief to Gratitude*, you will see how he turned his loss into purpose. He is beautifully honest with the feelings he uncovered. He lays it all out there for the reader; the highs and the lows of life and loss. Through it all, he recognizes the hand of God all along the way. Grief is not where you stop; it can actually be where a new path begins.

> Praise be to the God and Father of our Lord Jesus
> Christ, the Father of compassion and the God
> of all comfort, who comforts us in all our trou-

bles, so that we can comfort those in any trouble
with the comfort we ourselves receive from God.
(2 Corinthians 1:3–4)

Phil has taken his pain, his loss, his story, and is using it to comfort those who are on their own journey of grief. My prayer is that as you read this book, you will be blessed. I pray you also recognize that you are never alone.

—Heather Bean, Colead Pastor of Cowboy
Junction Church, Hobbs, New Mexico

PROLOGUE

Love is patient, love is kind, it does not envy, it does not boast,
it is not proud. It does not dishonor others, it is not self-seeking,
it is not easily angered, it keeps no record of wrongs. Love
does not delight in evil but rejoices with the truth. It always
protects, always trusts, always hopes, always perseveres.

—First Corinthians 13:4–7

Marlene and I were married in June of 1979, a lifetime ago. Our first date was just months earlier in November of 1978, on Thanksgiving weekend. I was working part-time while taking some college classes and had acquired season tickets to the Cincinnati Symphony through a student discount.

I would later discover this was not the type of music Marlene was surrounded with as a child, yet she seemed excited to attend the concert with me; and I believe she enjoyed the beautiful old-world style of the ornate Cincinnati Music Hall. Shortly after the music began, she fell asleep with her head resting on my shoulder.

On the ride back to Dayton, she abruptly changed the subject from the conversation we were having and asked me why I had asked her out. It was refreshing to be with someone who was so straight-forward, as I had found the games so often played in dating quite tedious. It always seemed there was an expectation I would be able to read the mind of my date. I think it was then I began to fall in love.

To my surprise, she agreed to go out with me again, and the next few dates were all at the Symphony. She always fell asleep. But she was an open book, frank and honest, and our conversations were long and left me wanting more. We quietly discussed marriage a few months later in February, thinking we would plan on a wedding in the fall or winter.

However, around that time, her father was diagnosed with cancer, and the prognosis wasn't promising. His health quickly showed signs of the struggle with the disease and chemo treatment. Marlene wanted him to be healthy enough to walk her down the aisle and to be able to enjoy the celebration. They had had a somewhat strained relationship over the years, but she did love him; and I could tell that in his own way, he loved her too. So we moved the marriage date up to June.

It was a simple wedding without much of the trappings and expensive options so often seen in today's American weddings, but that didn't diminish the joy or the love we were sharing and expressing. In later years, her family would remark that the pictures of her dad at our wedding were the last where he looked as they wanted to remember him, before the ravages of cancer took their toll on his physical appearance.

I have often said since then that we really had no business getting married—it seemed so financially irresponsible. Marlene was working full-time, and I had only a limited income and college expenses, yet we were so deeply in love. We doubled down on making our financial stress even greater by quickly deciding to try and start a family.

Marlene was the oldest of four and the first married. Her father's health continued to decline, and she wanted him to experience some hope for the future through a grandchild. When she became pregnant, it did seem to cheer him up; and in a quiet way, I believe it helped to bring them a bit closer. He passed away when she was five months pregnant.

I switched gears and began working full-time with taking just a class or two. I had been majoring in Business Administration, but through both high school and college, I had always minored in music. As music had always been my first passion, I began to instead focus on that for my classes.

We had grown up in a church with a strong music and worship tradition. It was large enough to afford me plenty of opportunities to participate and gain experience, and the minister of worship became a mentor for me. I continued studies in piano, organ, and voice, and worked to develop skills in writing and arranging.

Not long after our first son turned one year old, we were at church, listening to our pastor preach, and near the end of his sermon, he read from John.

> When they had finished eating, Jesus said to Simon Peter, "Simon son of John, do you love me more than these?"
>
> "Yes, Lord," he said, "you know that I love you."
>
> Jesus said, "Feed my lambs."

Again Jesus said, "Simon son of John, do you love me?"

He answered, "Yes, Lord, you know that I love you."

Jesus said, "Take care of my sheep." The third time he said to him, "Simon son of John, do you love me?" Peter was hurt because Jesus asked him the third time, "Do you love me?"

He said, "Lord you know all things; you know that I love you."

Jesus said, "Feed my sheep." (John 21:15–17)

Having grown up in the church, I had heard that passage used dozens of times in sermons and in various teaching venues, yet this time I was overwhelmed. It felt as though I was lifted out of my physical presence, and the ache in my heart and soul was deep and beyond any accurate description. Marlene sensed something was happening to me and reached over and grabbed my hand. I sat there, tears running down my face, wondering what God was trying to tell me.

Over the next few weeks, we prayed for God's guidance and for clarity. We came to the conclusion that God wanted us to commit to a full-time ministry, but we didn't understand exactly what type of ministry or where. Over the years, I came to appreciate that Marlene understood fully who I was, and many times, she expressed her support and belief that this was ultimately God's calling on my life.

There eventually were three times that we felt God touching us, leading me to a full-time ministry as an associate pastor. All three were successful in their own way, and in spite of my human shortcomings, He always blessed our efforts to reach out and lead the lives

He put in front of us and bring them closer to Him. However, the close of each ministry season seemed to always end poorly due to difficulties out of our control, and each left us financially drained. For one of these closures, Marlene was also going through a miscarriage, adding to the stress.

In later years, as we would reflect on those times, we never regretted following God's call, and we were thankful for the lessons learned and the wonderful people God brought into our path. Each time we would see that in spite of what someone on the outside would see as a bad experience, we instead saw how God used us for His purpose, and how ultimately, He would always provide exactly what we needed when we needed it.

There were times when we had no idea how to pay our bills, how to put food on the table for our two sons, or how to keep the lights on. At one point, when we were back in Ohio, my paternal grandfather had recently retired and was filling some of his time with a large vegetable garden. We lived near my grandparents and would often drop by to visit. We never openly talked about our situation, but my grandmother, whom I believe instinctively knew we were struggling, would always be sure that we had a big bag of potatoes and home-canned green beans to take home. This often would be the only thing we had to eat for a meal or two that week.

With God directing us, we crisscrossed the country several times, which meant frequent changes in jobs. Sometimes I had the primary income, for other times, it was Marlene; but for us, it didn't matter. We took comfort in knowing that we were in this together. I sometimes would worry that Marlene would resent me, as I was usually at the center of why we had to move or change careers, yet even with some occasional misgivings, she would always come through with support and love.

For reasons only fully known to God, after those three churches we worked at, there were no more opportunities for full-time ministry that came up. Although I sometimes felt a yearning to get back in the game, I always sensed an assurance from God that this was His plan. There were times I was able to help out with worship at whatever church we were attending, but as we kept moving, this was only sporadic. In any case, after all of the financial setbacks we had struggled through, it left me free to fully focus on taking care of Marlene and our sons, so perhaps this was at least part of the reason why.

> Two are better than one, because they have a
> good return for their labor: If either of them falls
> down, one can help the other up. But pity anyone
> who falls and has no one to help them up. Also,
> if two lie down together, they will keep warm.
> But how can one keep warm alone? Though one
> may be overpowered, two can defend themselves.
> A cord of three strands is not quickly broken.
> (Ecclesiastes 4:9–12)

It is often said that financial stress is one of the leading causes of marriage failures, but for us, it brought us closer. We became partners, shoulder to shoulder, committed to working together through whatever problems came our way, confident in God's provision. Marlene and I shared everything with each other, and it seemed as though there was a continuous conversation about whatever we were going through, our hopes and dreams, planning and praying along the way.

Over the years, not only did we grow closer but we also saw God's provision for us in truly amazing ways. I have often said that people would think we had more money than we actually did. While certainly not wealthy, we eventually came to live comfortably, with God blessing us with not only what we needed but with some extra blessings to enjoy as well. It became apparent to us that with each setback life gave us, God would ultimately bring even greater blessings. We grew in confidence and faith in God's protection so that when the next trial came, our resolve to depend on God was even stronger.

After so many battles fought, so many struggles endured, we eventually found ourselves approaching a point in life where we were looking forward to a more relaxed time together with retirement not far down the road. Our two sons were adults and gone, and we were now officially empty nesters; however, Marlene was beginning to experience issues with her health, and it seemed as though every year brought a new ailment.

As the chief cook for our family, I worked on modifying our meals to help deal with some of the conditions she had. I was very focused on taking care of her, as I wanted her to be as healthy as possible for the plans we had for the years ahead. To ease some of the physical stress on her, I took on more work to provide for us, which enabled her to pull back and work less. We just wanted to have enough money to enjoy our later years together, nothing more.

CHAPTER 1

Once Again

On Monday, August 23, 2021, I found myself in familiar yet unwelcome territory driving home from the hospital after spending all day there with Marlene.

This was the second time in less than two years where she was immediately admitted and with a prognosis that wasn't good. The first time was on Saturday, November 2, 2019, when I awoke to the sound of Marlene moaning in pain. Her discomfort was so severe that any movement of her legs would cause her to cry out from the pain. Her cries cut deep into my soul.

It was with great difficulty and the help of our younger son and the local police that I was able to get her to the ER. The medical staff gave her increasing doses of ever-stronger pain medication until morphine became the only, albeit somewhat limited, relief for her. After a number of tests, x-rays, and scans, it was determined she had a septic infection in her abdomen and left hip.

She was overdue for that hip to be replaced, something that had already been done to her right hip. She suffered from psoriatic arthritis, as well as a number of other issues that put her on immune-suppressant therapies. It was later determined that the infection possibly came from treatment for kidney stones some weeks earlier and likely was enhanced by the medications she was on.

She was in the ICU for several days, mostly because of the high doses of morphine needed to keep her marginally comfortable. At one point, while I was in the room alone with her, the morphine nearly took her life as her breathing and heart both slowed to a near stop, bringing on a series of alarms. When I looked up at the monitors and saw the numbers rapidly dropping, I rushed toward the door to see three of the medical staff running in to her side. Each took on a different task with multiple IVs being adjusted, injections being made, and one nurse leaning over to speak loudly in Marlene's ear, desperately trying to keep her conscious and, more importantly, alive.

At that moment, I believe my own heart stopped for a time, and I held my breath, almost as though in a dream state, watching these earthly angels rapidly working to save this life. Not sure what to do, I heard a familiar voice in my head and heart say, *Go.* Still not quite fully cognizant of all that was happening, but certainly not wanting to be in the way, I turned and walked out, eventually finding myself in a small outdoor courtyard. I sat on a bench and wept, asking God to intervene, to help the staff, to keep my life's partner alive. I wasn't ready to give her up, not yet.

At that time, we had been married forty years, yet regardless of her medical conditions, we were looking forward to our retirement years and growing old together. Our sons were not married, yet we were hopeful to eventually have some grandchildren to spoil. We dreamed of places we wanted to see and adventures to experience. Her mother had once described us as being "joined heart and hip," and we were truly partners in life's journey. Where one of us lacked or couldn't do, the other simply stepped in.

We talked over most every decision, even for some of the more mundane issues that came up. There was always support for each other, regardless of the situation, and even if one of us messed up or made a poor choice, there was not condemnation, just love. There were, of course, disagreements and the occasional argument, and I know I often got under her skin. The subject of cats as house pets was a common point of contention: she was a fan, but I wasn't. But ultimately, we were committed to each other, come what may.

Thankfully Marlene survived the scare, but the recovery was difficult on us both. After a couple of weeks in the hospital, she spent time in a rehab center before coming home and was subjected to IVs of high-powered antibiotics for weeks, with home health nurses coming and caring for her daily. The hip replacement was delayed for nearly a year, which meant she needed to use a walker or cane to get around. Even after the hip was finally replaced, she never regained her normal stride, and she found it difficult to walk much or stand for any length of time. She was always in pain.

Marlene had always worked and was a highly skilled executive assistant and paralegal, but now she found herself at home. She often expressed frustration that she could no longer work, but because of God's blessings, the loss of her pay was not an issue.

Just months before the septic infection hit, I was recruited by a company that had seen my profile on LinkedIn. Although I wasn't looking to make a career change at the time, it looked like an interesting new challenge. After both of us discussing the opportunity and prayer, I accepted the offer. At the time, I didn't fully understand why this had suddenly been made available to me, but now with Marlene unable to work, I recognized the much higher pay, benefits, and advancement opportunities for what they truly were. God was ahead of us and had already provided what we would need to make it through these new challenges.

After some discussion and assurance from me that we were financially secure, Marlene began to focus on the needs of others instead of earning a paycheck. Marlene was an excellent seamstress and loved various crafts, so she turned to using those skills to be a blessing. She made quilts and various items for nieces and nephews. She had an embroidery machine and made all sorts of items for others, often at no or little charge. When COVID hit, she worked for hours, day after day, making face masks for the local hospital that was desperately needing them for visitors, as they dealt with the initial supply shortages of those difficult times. She quietly found ways to touch the lives around her, often without them knowing. Always in pain, always with a kind smile.

That concept to be a blessing as the "hands and feet of Jesus" would come full circle down the road, with a deeper understanding of what it really meant.

While she was in recovery, I was studying Ephesians and found myself in chapter 5, where Paul talks of the relationship of wives and husbands. Paul's instructions to husbands in verse 25 seemed to really jump out at me:

Husbands, love your wives, just as Christ loved
the church and gave himself up for her. (Ephesians
5:25)

Given Marlene's health history, as well as that of her family, I always had it in the back of my mind that the odds were I'd outlive her. I did not want to dwell on this somber thought, but through His word, I knew God was telling me I needed to make some changes. I began to make some new and different decisions.

I accepted work opportunities I would not have previously, but with them came more pay and benefits to take care of Marlene and things at home. At one point, I took on an opportunity that nearly doubled my pay but initially required me to work out of town, leaving me home only on the weekends. Some of my hobbies were set aside: I sold my motorcycle, and I gave up having a piano, instead focusing on her needs. It was important for her to be comfortable with not working, to not be "contributing" to our bottom line, and to not feel that we were making a lot of sacrifices. We never discussed any of this, but after so many years of marriage, I knew that she knew what I was doing.

I could sense that God was teaching me to never assume there would be a tomorrow, to cherish every moment with her, to actively look for opportunities to show her I loved her. I'd like to say I always put these lessons to practice, but to be honest, I knew I could have done better. Still, I'm thankful for the lessons and opportunities God gave me to love her more.

So now, in spite of all of this, in spite of her past struggles and near-death experience, in spite of all that we had been through, here we were once again, facing another health crisis.

CHAPTER 2

The Prognosis

COVID. Not what I wanted to hear.

She had not been up to speed for a few days, commenting that she felt tired, a bit run down. In spite of me telling her that she really did not need to go back to work; she had just started back part-time for a school as an administrative assistant. As she didn't appear to have any other symptoms, my initial thought was that as she hadn't worked for nearly two years, her body just needed some time to adjust. She seemed to agree, but as the weekend progressed, so did her fatigue. As we often did for each other when one of us wasn't feeling well, on Sunday night, I slept out on my recliner so that she could get the best possible rest. After seeing her off to bed, I decided that if things didn't improve by morning, we'd head to the clinic to have her checked out.

I woke up early Monday morning to the sound of Marlene moaning. This was not a sound I had ever wanted to hear again, but there it was. When I entered our bedroom, I instantly knew from observing her that she was in trouble. She was still asleep, but it was obvious that she wasn't comfortable and was in some sort of distress. It was difficult to get her awake, and she was somewhat incoherent, struggling to understand and answer basic questions. My uneducated guess was lack of oxygen, which could only mean the one thing I had hoped would never come her way, especially with the potential comorbidity of her health issues and medications.

I helped her get dressed, as I saw that she was weak and not able to stand or walk on her own. When I told her that I was taking her to the ER, she insisted she just wanted to go to the local clinic, but I made it clear she had no choice in the matter. When we got there, she was immediately admitted and tested, with the results confirming my fears.

Thankfully, the hospital let me spend the day with her in ER until a regular hospital room was made available. That evening, after running home to feed the critters and take a quick shower, I received a call from the hospitalist who was caring for her.

Her prognosis was very negative. Her condition was quite poor, as the disease had rapidly progressed to the point that treatment was little more than a hope God could do the rest. Three of the medications she was on along with her health problems put her at higher risk. She needed an ICU bed along with the attendant advanced care it would bring, but none were available in a five-state region. There was little they could do, but whatever they could, they would. By his tone of voice, I could tell the next part of the conversation was not going to be easy.

He wanted to know if she had a living will or anything to indicate her wishes should she be incapacitated. Although in recent years I had been bugging her to update our will and other such legal documents, she had always resisted, changing the subject. He told me that as her condition was so poor, the hospital wanted to know if I would indicate my directions for them should her condition degrade to the point where she would not be able to provide her wishes on her own.

After this quick assessment of her condition, he hinted that perhaps I might want to come down to meet him face-to-face and possibly sign a DNR (Do Not Resuscitate), and I agreed. The emotions that evening at the hospital were so mixed, wildly swinging from one point to the next. I was directly faced with the strong probability of losing her; I was having to make the decision whether to let her go should that time come, but on the bright side, the hospitalist did let me go in to see her briefly after some pretty serious suiting up.

Driving home that evening, many emotions roared to the surface: grief, then frustration, then anger. Especially anger. Although some of my anger was directed at Marlene due to my frustration with her not always doing a good job of taking care of herself, the full depth of my emotion was directed at God. Over the years, our lives had been turned upside down so many times with unexpected events: job and career changes, opportunities blocked, dreams shattered, finances destroyed. We had moved eleven times in those forty-two years, several of those cross-country, most often at what we felt was God's direction. It seemed as though every time the dust settled and we sensed a clear path ahead of us, something in our lives would blow up, once again putting us in a state of uncertainty and confusion.

Having lived through those times, I had developed a bit of a tough skin, learning to "roll with the punches," quickly adapting to each new situation, looking to God for direction and peace. But this was a bridge too far. I was really pissed and found myself yelling at God. I felt picked on. *Just once, could we live our lives in peace? We have suffered so many setbacks, and she has suffered so much pain. Can we simply be left alone to enjoy a quiet, peaceful life? Retirement is only a few years away. What of our hopes, our plans, our desires?*

By the time I got home, I had a pretty strong head of steam built up and paced the floor for a while, fuming over what was happening to Marlene, to us. When I finally settled into my recliner, my eyes caught a glimpse of my Bible sitting on the end table next to me, or more specifically, I was looking at the cover on my Bible. On it is inscribed a verse from Jeremiah:

> "For I know the plans I have for you," declares the
> Lord, "plans to prosper you and not to harm you,

plans to give you hope and a future." (Jeremiah
29:11)

I initially responded in anger. *How could her suffering and her potential death be prosperity and not harm? How would that give me hope, or a future to look forward to?* My eyes kept landing on that Bible cover, on that verse in Jeremiah. Finally, remembering there was more to that passage, I opened my Bible to that verse and read on:

> Then you will call upon me and come and pray
> to me, and I will listen to you. You will seek me
> and find me when you seek me with all your
> heart. (Jermiah 29:12–13)

But God… "Seek me." But God… "Trust me." Okay, God, but please bring Marlene back to me. We have so much life to live. I know that our plans are only good when they exist in Your plans, but please, I'm not ready to lose her. I'm not strong enough to handle that kind of great disruption and loss in my life.

Silence. I sat in silence for what seemed forever, as I continued to plead with God to preserve her life, to allow us to continue to share our love for each other. Still the silence. Totally drained, I went to bed, no longer able to think or contemplate what tomorrow would bring. I was beaten. As I began to drift off, the silence broke with a voice quietly and clearly saying: *She's mine. Let her go.*

CHAPTER 3

Decisions

I woke up the next morning feeling surprisingly rested, calm, and refreshed. I busied myself with the process of notifying and updating family and friends on what was happening, asking everyone to be praying for her.

Through all of these conversations, I tried to find a balance of admitting how desperate her situation was but to also express that she was now in God's hands. I believed that He was fully capable of healing her. I never told anyone at the time what the Holy Spirit had told me the night before, or what I feared it may mean. I honestly did and do still believe in God's healing power and had witnessed His miraculous interventions on a number of occasions. But how He would choose to heal her in this crisis was as yet unseen.

A video chat with our two sons was particularly difficult, as I had to be very honest about what may be coming. Through it all, I tried to play the part of the strong one, but inside I was in turmoil. Our older son was stationed overseas in the military, and at his instruction, I contacted the Red Cross so he would qualify for emergency leave.

The strict COVID restrictions at the time meant I could only "visit" Marlene from outside, looking through her hospital window. This was not an easy feat due to the dense landscaping packed with mosquitoes and, at midday, the incredibly hot New Mexico sun. Morning and evening visits with lots of insect repellent became the norm. We did our best to communicate with hand motions, but I longed instead to hold her hands, to be with her and comfort her. Our younger son lived an hour and a half away, yet he made regular visits to see her. He also made it a point to keep checking on me to see how I was doing, for which I was very grateful.

After a couple of days, her condition improved slightly, giving all of us a deeper hope that in spite of all the headwinds she was facing, perhaps recovery would be possible. I believe we all doubled down on our prayers, asking God to step in and heal her.

The respite was short-lived, however, as a day later her condition began to rapidly deteriorate. I noticed her hands were swollen, and the doctor told me that they were now dealing with kidney issues, among other things, and were struggling to keep her bodily fluids in check. With the swelling, she couldn't hold anything, and I could tell she was getting frustrated with her situation. At this point, she wasn't always awake when I'd visit, and over the next couple of days, it was obvious things weren't going well, as I could detect physical changes with each visit, even through the heavily tinted window.

On Sunday, while my son and I were outside her window for a visit, the hospitalist called to see if we could talk. Discovering that we were there, he and the doctor who was caring for her came out for a face-to-face discussion. The doctor told us that they were losing not only the COVID battle in her lungs, but that the situation with her kidneys was becoming increasingly difficult to manage. They didn't say it directly, but my son and I both knew what was being said.

There still was no opportunity for an ICU unit, and quite honestly, her health had deteriorated to the point that she probably would not survive transport. The only outside chance they saw was to put her in intubation, essentially putting her "on hold" as best they could on the dim possibility that an ICU and advanced care would become available. But again, transport would be difficult, at best. And it would also be quite possible she would never make it out of intubation.

Since she was still awake and coherent, the choice of what to do would be hers, but they wanted us to fully understand what the situation was and also wanted to know how I felt. I told them I didn't want to lose her, but even more so, I didn't want to cling to her, extending the suffering she was currently experiencing. Our son nodded and agreed. A few hours later, they explained everything to her and then called me on speakerphone so that I could be part of the conversation.

By that time, I was back home. It was a heart-wrenching experience beyond description. I did my best, but I couldn't help but sob as I told her that I loved her and I didn't want to lose her, nor did I want to make her suffer. The decision was hers, and I would support whatever she chose. Her lungs were so filled and incapacitated that she could barely talk, gasping out a few words in between someone there giving her oxygen. She said she felt she didn't have any choice and wanted the intubation. The hospitalist asked if I understood, and I said I did.

She then said, "Take care of my kitties."

I responded, "Already on it, babe."

Neither one of us could bring ourselves to actually say goodbye, but after forty-two years of marriage, we knew it was what we meant.

The next few days, I kept myself as busy as best I could, cleaning and recleaning the house, finding odd chores to do out in the yard and garage. As intubation required Marlene to be sedated and I couldn't actually see her, I stopped going to the hospital, instead spending that same time in the morning and evening praying and asking God for intervention for her and strength for me. I would periodically call the nurse's desk to see if there were any updates.

In my home office above my desk, there is a picture of an eagle with a reverence to a passage in Isaiah.

> He gives strength to the weary and increases the power of the weak. Even youths grow tired and weary, and young men stumble and fall; but those who hope in the Lord will renew their strength. They will soar on wings like eagles; they will run and not grow weary, they will walk and not be faint. (Isaiah 40:29–31)

With all of the setbacks and problems I had faced over the years, this had become a favorite scripture of mine, a promise from God I clung to in times of trouble. All of what had happened in the past paled to what I was now facing. I prayed to God, repeated my desire to understand that she was in His hands, and pleaded with Him to heal her and give me whatever I needed to make it through each day, come what may.

I was out by the garage, changing the oil on my truck, when my phone rang. It was the doctor. He was giving me an update on her condition, but I could tell there was an unspoken question he had for me. Her kidneys were failing, there were no ICU rooms available, and her condition had become quite dire. I asked him, "So what you are telling me is we're fighting a losing battle?" After a brief pause, he said yes. I then told him I didn't see any point in prolonging the agony she was going through, and that we were done. He said he understood and that I would be contacted when the time came to take her out of intubation.

Since I was a mess from working on the vehicles, I ran inside to quickly clean up. As I got out of the shower, a nurse called and said they were ready to take her out of intubation, and they wanted to know if I wanted to be there with her as she passed. The invitation to be there was a surprise, given the current COVID restrictions. I was about to say yes, but instead I took a moment to think.

In what could only be described as another "God-incident," a few months earlier I had bought airline tickets to Ohio to visit my parents in September. That flight to Ohio was now a week away, perfect timing for meeting with both of our families for some type of memorial for Marlene. Could I, in good conscience, travel to visit my parents, at that time in their late eighties—let alone the rest of the family—if I went to Marlene and potentially be exposed to COVID? Our older son was currently in the air, flying home on emergency leave. International travel had quite strict COVID rules. If I went into the hospital, would that expose him or otherwise jeopardize his ability to travel back to Japan?

My heart sank as I explained to the nurse my situation and that I couldn't come in. It was time to think of the future, of those who would still be living. I asked her if Marlene would wake when taken out of intubation. She said it occasionally happens, but not always. So I requested that they make sure she stayed sedated. I didn't want her to wake up and be confused, or to experience any suffering when she would be taken out of intubation. The nurse said she understood.

I threw on my clothes and drove down to the hospital. Even though I could not be in the room with her to hold her hand, to tell her God was waiting for her, I had a strong desire to be there. On the way down, I asked God to be with her, to comfort her, and to also give me strength. Arriving, I parked the car, and as I got out, my phone rang. It was the nurse. Marlene had already passed away. The nurse assured me it was quiet and peaceful.

CHAPTER 4

Details

Over the years, I had witnessed the many different ways people seem to process loss.

For me, at least initially, I felt numb. I was thankful for the distraction of all the details that had to be so quickly dealt with. There were to be simple gatherings at our church in New Mexico, as well as at what could be described as our home church in Ohio. With COVID restrictions and with a need to avoid close gatherings, especially for my son flying in from Japan, both churches were able to provide ideal open spaces, for which I was incredibly grateful.

There was not going to be a formal funeral, so I gathered pictures of Marlene, our wedding album, and had newer pictures of her printed and framed, all to be displayed for folks to see and remember her by. After the New Mexico gathering, I air shipped these memories to Ohio. While there, I made sure Marlene's three siblings were able to pick out and take with them pictures that they wanted for remembrance.

I had always been a bit of a control freak, and with all of my managerial experience, I had long ago developed the ability to compartmentalize my emotions from whatever task was at hand. For those first two very busy weeks, I was often able to play the part of strength through the numbness.

On the flights home to New Mexico, at the end of all of this activity, I began creating a mental checklist of all the tasks that still needed to be taken care of. It made me happy to have so much to do and not have to stop and think about Marlene and how much I already missed her. I was also looking forward to the distraction of spending some time with my two sons while my older son was home from Japan. The next morning at home, during my Bible study, I was reading in Psalms:

> So my spirit grows faint within me; my
> heart within me is dismayed.
> I remember the days of long ago: I meditate on all your works
> and consider what your hands have done.
> I spread out my hands to you; my soul
> thirsts for you like a parched land.
> Answer me quickly, O Lord; my spirit fails.
> Do no hide your face from me or I will be
> like those who go down to the pit.
> Let the morning bring me word of your unfailing
> love, for I have put my trust in you.
> Show me the way I should go, for to you I lift up my soul.
> (Psalm 143:4–8)

I stopped. In all of my attention to details, not only had I compartmentalized my emotions, but I had also shut out God. I broke down and pleaded with God to forgive me, for being so arrogant to think I could handle this on my own. So what was to come next? How would I deal with the loss and grief I was doing my best to avoid facing? Where was God's comfort for me? What were His plans for me? The rest of the day, I kept busy; but now with these questions running through my mind, I wanted answers, and now.

I thought back to our second ministry, which was actually overseas. The boys were in early elementary grades, so it was quite a step of faith to sell our house, cars, and many of our possessions to make the move. The assignment revealed itself to be very different than what we had originally thought, as I found myself in the role of seeing the church through a transition of both leadership and focus. As an expat in a foreign country, I was on an annually renewable work permit. At a point where this renewal was coming up, I met with the leadership, and we made the decision that with a new pastor in place and the church moving forward on a new path, my task was complete and it was time to leave.

I remember going home that evening, and Marlene and I both shed some tears at the thought of leaving these people whom we had come to love so much. With a young family, we now faced having to leave this ministry by the end of my work permit in two months with no idea as to where we would go or what we would end up doing for income. After some prayer, we almost simultaneously and suddenly felt a peace come over us. We talked about how God had always come through for us, and we knew He would again.

The next morning, while I was getting ready to go into the office, I received a phone call from a pastor back in the States. He told me he didn't know if I was looking to make a move but that he had been referred to me as someone with the unique combination of skills his church was looking for: music and business. After interviews, visits, and many conversations, we ended up moving to work at that church. God was, once again, way ahead of us. It turned out to be another difficult yet very rewarding ministry, with people I will never forget.

Now, reminding myself of all the times like this when God had come through for me, for us, the times I knew He was already in whatever situation I found myself in, I came to a sense of calm. In His time and in His way, He would reveal what was to come, and I would simply have to wait for His reply. Meanwhile, the weight of loss and grief was heavy on my soul.

The next morning as I woke, I looked up at a framed print I have on the wall next to my bed. On it is a passage from Proverbs:

> Trust in the Lord with all your heart and lean not on your own understanding; in all your ways acknowledge him, and he will make your paths straight. (Proverbs 3:5–6)

Okay, so let's say I do this. I trust You to help me with the grief, to discover what comes next. What does that mean, really? How will I discover what You mean by this?

All day I struggled with this promise of God, as this scripture and all my questions kept running through my head. It was difficult to fall asleep that night, but as often happened, it was when I finally shut down and quieted my heart and brain that I could once again sense the voice of Holy Spirit: *Turn the page.*

Now new questions ran through my mind. What exactly did this mean? How would this play out? I was familiar with this phrase, as over the years for me, it came to represent an important inflection point each time I faced some dramatic change in my life. To "turn the page" came to mean that things would change, that what was the past would remain in the past, that there was now a new path and new challenges to be faced. Just as it had so many years earlier when it came time for us to leave that church overseas, it always meant a step of faith in God's will, His wisdom, His provision.

Without the life partner God had so blessed me with, I missed Marlene dearly. In times like this, we would talk and pray together, striving to sense what God was telling us. But now the loss of the closeness of our relationship fully demonstrated itself as I experienced the depth of how alone I felt without her. I wrestled with all of this as I drifted off to sleep, wondering just how this next chapter of my life would play out.

CHAPTER 5

Discoveries

Late the next morning, a friend of mine, who had lost his spouse a few years earlier, stopped by to check up on me and pass on some of his experience and advice.

I mostly listened and nodded and deeply appreciated his concern and support. At one point, I couldn't help but smile a bit as he was suggesting to me that it would be best to not yet make any major decisions and allow some time for me to first adjust to my loss. Thanking him and giving him a hug as he left, I mentioned that all of us have different life experiences and are wired differently, and that his visit was very welcome.

Earlier that morning, as I woke up, I remembered a story I had heard many years ago in a sermon. Decades later, I'm sure I have some of the details wrong, but the message it relayed was still very clear in my mind. I believe it was about some Wycliffe Bible Translators who were in a remote jungle working to understand the language of a group of indigenous people. Wycliffe has a mission to learn a language so that they can translate the Bible for a people who have never learned of God's love. Sometimes this entails creating a written form for a language for the first time.

In this story, the translators were struggling with how to translate the concept of faith, as there was no word for it in this particular language. One day while spending time with these people, they were to transverse a rickety rope bridge over a ravine. A local volunteer crossed the bridge to test it, and when he got to the other side, he yelled back, "Put your whole weight on it!" This phrase became the concept used to relay the idea of faith in the Bible they would translate and create for this people.

I understood that God was now asking me to do the same, to trust and have faith in His provision and ability to heal my heart. It was time to put my life more deeply in His hands and venture into a new future.

After some reflection and prayer, I called my general manager and told him that I was not returning to work and instead would be taking an early retirement. This was particularly difficult for several reasons. I had come to understand that the opportunity of working for this company was truly a gift from God, as it had provided all we needed while Marlene was going through such a difficult time.

I enjoyed a good relationship with my manager and was deeply moved when he drove nearly five hours to visit and pay his respects at the memorial gathering for Marlene in New Mexico. He had also been very kind and patient with me as I was dealing with Marlene's hospitalization, death, and the time I needed to travel to Ohio and back.

Financially, it made zero sense for me to quit. Because of some of the hardships we had endured over the years, I didn't have much in the way of investments or retirement income to fall back on. There certainly would not be enough to live on, and travel (something I loved to do) would be totally out of the question. Besides, I was relatively young, still healthy; and with a family history of longevity, it was safe to assume I still had many years of activity and productivity in my future. My upbringing had ingrained in me a tradition of keeping active and to always be at some task or another, so I really didn't see myself happy just sitting around in some type of quiet and passive retirement.

Regardless, I felt strongly this change was part of God's plan, that it was time to start a new life with a clean slate. As a person who always liked to think ahead and have a plan, I was strangely very much at peace with this decision. I thought about the passage in Matthew where Jesus teaches us to not worry but to focus instead on the correct priority.

> Therefore I tell you, do not worry about your life, what you will eat or drink; or about your body, what you will eat. Is not life more important than food, and the body more important than clothes? Look at the birds of the air; they do not sow or reap or store away in barns, and yet your heavenly Father feeds them. Are you not much more valuable than they? Who of you by worrying can add a single hour to his life? (Matthew 6:25–27)

> But seek first his kingdom and his righteousness, and all these things will be given to you as well. (Matthew 6:33)

So later in that morning, while my friend was telling me to be patient before making major decisions, I was smiling as I realized how, once again, God's timing is impeccable. If I had heard my friend's advice earlier, I don't know if I would have made the same choice. There was nothing wrong with my friend's counsel, for to many, if not most, in my situation, it may be wise to consider what he shared with me.

Paul speaks in 1 Corinthians 12 how we as followers of Christ are of one body but many different parts:

> But in fact God has arranged the parts in the body, every one of them, just as he wanted them

> to be. If they were all of one part, where would
> the body be? As it is, there are many parts, but
> one body. (1 Corinthians 12: 17–20)

As Paul continues to expand and explain on this theme, in chapter 14 he speaks to how we are each equipped with different gifts to fulfill different functions. I've come to see that in any given situation, God may ask us to respond differently according to His will and plan for our individual lives. We will not all have the same path, but we all have the same Guide.

After my friend left, I found myself walking through the house. Marlene seemed to be everywhere I looked, with some things bringing a smile of a fond memory, yet others bringing on a deep sense of sadness. With the thought of "turning the page" in mind, I decided that while I had some time to discover God's plans for me, I would keep myself busy clearing the clutter, something that always seemed to raise my blood pressure anyway.

Marlene had always been a pack rat, finding it difficult to throw away anything. She couldn't resist what she felt was a bargain; and with her love of sewing and various crafts, she had built up a huge stock pile in her sewing room, so much so that it was difficult to even walk through the room. The large kitchen—with ample cabinets, drawers, and a pantry—was stuffed full of far more food and gadgets than two people could ever need. The refrigerator was the same. She had two walk-in closets packed with clothes, most of which were either out of style or the wrong size. The garage, workshop, and attic were overflowing with storage bins full of sewing and crafting supplies that hadn't been touched in years.

I had often laughed and kidded her that if she had not been married to me, she would have made a great candidate for the TV show that featured hoarders. So being a planner and methodical even in difficult times, I began to formulate an attack plan, creating and prioritizing lists of things to go through, things to change at home.

Through the years, I know of many who have suffered loss who needed time and healing before they could go through the personal belongings of their loved one. For me, however, it seemed to make sense as part of my healing process to instead dig in and do it right away. I felt I needed to physically and emotionally experience the closure of seeing my surroundings change. I would always miss her and want to cling to the wonderful memories, but I was not going to live in a shrine. There had to be a balance found.

After creating and reediting the lists several times, I found myself sitting and staring at the plans I had written down. Tears came to my eyes, and I was frozen in place. Grief overwhelmed me, and something else came to the fore that surprised me: immense guilt.

CHAPTER 6

The Accusation

The next several days were difficult, at best, and sleep didn't come easily.

I agonized over every decision I had made over the forty-two years of our marriage, especially in the last several years. I questioned my motivations, ran through what seemed to me infinite what ifs of choices made. Here I was, having lost the very person who was my life's partner, my right arm, my confidant, the mother of my sons. How could I dare to be looking forward to a new life? A recent memory came back to haunt me.

A few months before Marlene had passed away, when I was still working out of town, I was home for the weekend. We had a somewhat heated discussion while eating dinner when I had discovered Marlene was skipping a much-needed medication because of the high cost. I was upset with her for not taking care of herself, and hurt that she felt we couldn't afford it. This was not the case, but her decision came from years of us having frequent financial struggles, forcing us to develop a habit to be as frugal as possible. I assured her that with our current income and insurance we could handle it and pleaded with her to never again hide anything like this from me.

After dinner, I took the dog for a walk, still upset and frustrated. I was working out of town, living out of a suitcase and not home with my love, nor was I there helping to take care of her. And to make matters worse, her health continued to decline. I remember a thought popped up in my head, one that I never thought possible: *Wouldn't it be so much easier without her?*

From the depths of my heart I knew this wasn't true to my love for her, but where did this evil thought come from? Asking God for forgiveness and continuing my walk, I eventually came to realize that this was evidence of just how frustrated I was with our situation.

So now this memory comes roaring back, and with her gone, I began to question every decision, everything I had done leading up to her death. Should I have been more cautious and taken her to the hospital sooner? What was my motivation to sign the DNR and eventually tell the doctor that there was no more to be done? Why did I feel so much relief once she passed away? Why did I seem actually happy and looking forward to "turning the page"? After all the times I was angry with her for not taking better care of herself, was I blaming her for my current situation, especially after discovering that she actually had several COVID symptoms but had never shared them with me? Were all of these plans somehow an effort to erase Marlene from my life, from my memories?

All of these questions and more tore me apart in a never-ending loop that seemed to drag me further into guilt and despair. And to make my situation worse, I didn't have her there with me as I had for forty-two years to listen to me, to counsel me, to love me, to pray with me, and to tell me it would all be okay.

After a few days of this agony, my son called to check up on me and to invite himself over for dinner. The distraction was much needed, and it gave me an excuse to get out of the house to shop for a few things for our meal and run a few errands. While in one of the stores, I bumped into a former coworker with whom I had enjoyed a pretty good relationship. He knew about Marlene, and asked me how I was doing. I told him there were good days, and bad, but that currently I was dealing with some guilt, as I was realizing I felt relief and was looking forward to a new life. He smiled and told me this wasn't unusual.

Although we had always been friendly and worked well together, when we were coworkers we didn't normally get deeply personal in our conversations. What I didn't know until talking to him on this occasion was that he had once done some work with hospice. He told me that it was common for folks who have lost a loved one after any lengthy struggle to feel relief, but more importantly, he told me that the guilt was common as well. He assured me that I should in fact feel relief, as Marlene was now no longer suffering, and God had lifted the burden of her earthly care from my shoulders. This was not something to feel guilty for.

I walked away amazed and thankful for this "God-incident," but my heart was still struggling. Was it all so simple as this? And what of all the other decisions, the choices I made?

That evening after dinner, my son and I took the dog for a walk. I shared with him my struggles with guilt, that I believed God had a new path ahead of me, but that I wondered if somehow I was being unfaithful or dishonoring his mom. I was questioning the decisions I made to sign the DNR and tell the doctor we needed to let her go. He turned to me and told me I had nothing to feel guilty about. He said that because of the care I had given her over the years, the meals I adjusted to meet her needs, and the changes I made in my job to provide better pay and insurance, he believed, if anything, I had probably extended her life. I was glad it was already dark, as tears fell from my eyes.

The next couple of days were better, and even though I still didn't know what God had in store for me, I decided that just sitting around was certainly not what He wanted. It was time to begin the process of turning the page to eventually discover God's plan for me. The feelings of guilt and grief were still fresh, and there were times I could sense the darkness once again coming over me. If God wanted me to feel relief and wanted me to look forward to how He would now use me, where do these powerful negative emotions come from, and why do they have such a strong hold?

I remembered learning some years ago that the Hebrew word *Satan* can be translated as "Accuser." While the Holy Spirit will speak to us about things in our lives that need correction, it is Satan who will try to discourage us and keep our focus on anything other than God by lying to us and hounding us with distortions of the truth. Revelation tells us that until God's final victory, while we are still on earth, this is a never-ending battle we must acknowledge and face:

> Then I heard a loud voice in heaven say: "Now have come the salvation and the power and the kingdom of our God, and the authority of his Christ. For the accuser of our brothers, who accuses them before our God day and night, has been hurled down." (Revelation 12:10)

I realized that for me, and possibly many of us going through the pain of loss and grief, Satan can use these accusations, these what ifs, and these doubts to freeze us in place, always questioning and feeling guilty for our actions and motives. Deep in my heart and soul, I knew that God had plans for me, and I also knew that I never wavered in my love for Marlene and my desire for the best for her. If I allowed Satan to distract me, I would never complete whatever tasks God had for me. I would never again experience the peace and joy that comes with living in God's will.

It was then that I also realized that grief should be something you journey through; it is not someplace to live in. While I knew I would always feel a sense of loss and miss Marlene, I began to understand that with God, there is always strength, and there is always a hope and a future.

> I remember my affliction and my wandering, the bitterness and the gall. I well remember them, and my soul is downcast within me. Yet this I call to mind and therefore I have hope: Because of the Lord's great love we are not consumed, for his compassions never fail. They are new every morning; great is your faithfulness. I say to myself, "The lord is my portion; therefore I will wait for him. The lord is good to those whose hope is in him, to the one who seeks him." (Lamentations 3:21–25)

CHAPTER 7

Choices

Every journey of grief is different, but for me, after a couple of months, it felt like it was time for me to fully embrace my new life without Marlene.

Of course, I would always remember and miss her, but I was determined to move forward down whatever path God had in store for me. I revisited the lists I had created earlier of tasks and changes around the house that needed to be done, made a few edits, and set priorities.

The thought of potentially having a massive garage sale ran through my mind, but I couldn't resolve all of the practical aspects of an undertaking of that type, especially by myself. Although the money it would generate would have been welcome, I just didn't have it in my heart to see money as the priority. We had very little debt when Marlene passed away, but I also didn't have much in the way of life insurance payments or other investments to live on. Regardless, I decided to lean on God's provision and trust Him to show me how to fill in the financial blanks. I also made the decision to continue tithing, even though my current income was insufficient. I had learned long ago that I could never out give God.

Give generously to them [the poor] and do so without a grudging heart; then because of this the Lord your God will bless you in all your work and in everything you put your hand to. There will always be poor people in the land. Therefore I command you to be openhanded toward your fellow Israelites who are poor and needy in your land. (Deuteronomy 15:10–11)

And so the work began. Truckloads of clothes went to charity, and a stash of fabric with prints suitable for children was given to a local group who made quilts for every kindergartner in our small local school.

In another "God-incident," I was able to connect with a woman who was willing to do a limited estate sale of the embroidery and other sewing machines as well as the huge supply of sewing and crafting goods, with the understanding that for me, money was not the main concern, and anything left over could be given to charity.

Getting all of this to her entailed a large amount of work, and I stopped counting at seven truckloads cleared out from Marlene's sewing room, eventually moving on to find even more stored in the garage and attic. I had to chuckle several times, as it seemed as though there was some type of magic involved. Every time I thought I had it all, I would find more.

At this point, a fond memory came to me from when we were moving overseas. We were limited in what we could take with us for the move there, and Marlene was concerned about taking her sewing machine and the large stash of supplies and material she had built up.

Reminding her of the restrictions we were working with, I told her that for the fabric she would have to narrow it down to one box. Anything else would have to be sold or stored for later use. At the time, I could only laugh when I later discovered she had used the biggest box she could find and had it tightly packed. The box was so heavy; it took two strong men from the moving company, red-faced with the strain, to carry it out. More than once while we lived there, I would laugh and tease Marlene that she had more material on hand than the small local fabric store that was there on the island.

The kitchen came next, and I began to get into a rhythm of enjoying many great memories of life with my wonderfully unique Marlene. I also found some surprises that, knowing her as well as I did, probably shouldn't have surprised me so much.

A few years earlier, as the main cook and baker in the family, I had bought some new baking sheets to replace some old ones that were well past their prime. The new ones were washed and put into place, and I put the old ones out in the trash. Now while going through the kitchen cabinets, there were the old baking sheets that she had retrieved from the trash tucked in the back so that I wouldn't see them! I laughed so hard I was near tears.

I still had moments when the loss would grip me. I would walk into a room to see something she had made, or turn to tell her something that was on my mind only to feel that emptiness in my heart as I once again realized she wasn't there. I knew being by myself with the dog and cats was an adjustment that was going to take some time; however, I recalled in Psalms a number of passages where the psalmist would be crying out to God, itemizing whatever suffering or loss he was experiencing.

Then abruptly, the psalmist would change to praising God for His love and provision, as if to remember that even in the darkest times we will always have hope in God. Psalms 42 and 43 demonstrate this characteristic clearly, pleading with God for deliverance but then repeatedly injecting this refrain:

> Why are you so downcast, O my soul?
> Why so disturbed within me?
> Put your hope in God,
> for I will yet praise him,
> my Savior and my God.
> (Psalm 42:11–12)

It was then that a thought began to rattle around in the back of my mind, not quite fully formed, not quite yet fully understood. I was beginning to sense the Holy Spirit teaching me that there was plenty of room in my heart to both enjoy the fond memories of my forty-two years with Marlene and to also look forward to and celebrate what God had in store for me. I was thankful for the blessing of God, giving me such a wonderful partner over those years, but now I was beginning to realize I needed to focus on praising God not only for where He had led me in the past but also for where He had yet to take me. To do this involved daily making choices to lean more on God's guidance and provisions.

It was now early November, and God continued to teach me lessons on making choices, sometimes in very unexpected ways. While out doing some shopping and errands, I was in our local Hobby Lobby and noticed they already had their Christmas items out. Christmas had always been a highlight of the year for me, and I admit to loving putting up the tree and decorations.

Outside, the house was always well lit, and I must confess to the sin of pride in the display I put on yet did my best to not fall into a tacky, over-the-top Griswold trap. I instead chose to focus on beauty and celebration. No elves or other more secular decorations were to be found on my yard. Instead, a nativity was the centerpiece. I always felt, and still do, that I wanted the outside display at my house to not only be a gift to the community, but to also be a gentle reminder of what the celebration of this season was truly about.

So still feeling like I needed some positive reinforcement to my mood, I decided to browse through the Christmas decorations they had and see if there was anything I just "had to have." While walking through the store, I came across a display of nutcrackers of various styles, colors, and sizes. One in particular caught my eye and was soon in my shopping cart. At two-and-a-half feet, it was the largest one they had.

Marlene loved *The Nutcracker* ballet. When we lived in the city, at Christmas time we usually went to see the performance by the local ballet company. After we moved to rural New Mexico, seeing a live performance was no longer a possibility. So for one of our first years there at Christmas, I bought her a very good HD Blu-ray copy of it. Part of our Christmas routine every year after that was to watch it in our recliners, snuggled under blankets with a fire in the fireplace.

I looked down at the nutcracker in my cart with a big smile, knowing the exact spot by the fireplace it would be placed, and I admit my eyes got a bit misty. A friend of mine walked up and said hello and wondered how I was doing. She remarked on the rather large nutcracker in my cart and how pretty it was. Then she spoke about how difficult it was likely to be for me with the upcoming holiday season, as it is often said the first year of holidays are pretty tough for those who have lost a spouse or anyone close.

While listening to her and nodding, I remembered hearing a pastor once saying that our attitude is our choice. While this is a fairly simple statement regarding a very complex issue, in my current circumstance I had come to understand the kernel of truth behind it more than ever before. I told her, "You know, I've heard that too. But with God's grace, this Christmas I choose joy." I'm not sure which of us was more surprised at my statement, but she smiled and said she'd be praying for me as she walked away.

My next stop was at Lowe's to pick up a few things I needed for projects I was planning for the house, and of course, they also had their Christmas items out. Now beginning to feel a bit more upbeat, I just had to see what they had to offer. After viewing some of the interior decorations and some of the latest new lighting options, I came to where the outside decorations were. I stood with my eyes once again misting up as I stared at what I knew I had to buy and prominently place in front of my house that Christmas. Before me were three large lit red letters for display in the yard: "J-O-Y."

CHAPTER 8

Moving on

With the holidays approaching and given my Swiss/German heritage and proclivities, I knew that I needed to get a fair amount of work done to get the house sufficiently tidied before the holidays actually came.

In my thinking, this would then allow me to zero-in on the celebrations of the season, something that I instinctively knew I would need if I had any hope of making it through without falling in to a deeper sense of grief.

I still had times that the realization of now being alone would hit me pretty hard, and to be honest, I wasn't looking forward to the next phase of going through the house, as it would now be more focused on some of the more personal and meaningful items. I prayed that God would show me how to maneuver through what I feared could be a dangerous minefield of emotions.

With time and practice, and sensing guidance from the Holy Spirit, I developed a habit of viewing things through a lens of how they made me feel. If an object brought good memories and a smile, I would consider keeping it. If it in anyway made me feel sad or deepen my sense of loss, it likely was something that would go. I suppose this routine became part of the healing process, as I learned over time to focus more on the good times and happy memories. I also decided that there would be some things about the house and decor I would change so that the house felt more like my house yet still give me opportunities to relish fond memories of life with Marlene.

An example of this was in the bedroom. I got rid of the rather feminine floral quilt on the bed and replaced it with one that was much more neutral, if not a bit masculine, in design. The lace bed skirt and curtains were replaced as well. I hung up my grandfather's antique 1930 Winchester .22 rifle he had purchased in the midst of the Great Depression to hunt rabbits and squirrels. But on the bookcase headboard, I kept a cross-stitch that Marlene had made of a peacock. Above the bed, I left a pair of paintings of hummingbirds I had given her on our fortieth anniversary.

She loved the hummers, and I kept a couple of feeders going for them during the summer, hung in places where she could easily see them while outside resting on the deck or inside recouping on her recliner. I still keep those feeders going and often smile and think of her while watching their acrobatics. When I was done with the bedroom, it was decidedly more to my taste, and it reflected me in new ways, but more importantly, it still included my life with and my love for Marlene.

Increasingly, I was thinking about what I would do next for income. It had been a step of faith to go ahead and retire early. Although I remained convinced it was the right decision, I have to admit to becoming increasingly anxious about what I would do to both keep busy and pay the bills. One morning, I read from Psalms:

> Show me your ways, Lord,
> teach me your paths.
> Guide me in your truth and teach me,
> for you are God my Savior
> and my hope is in you all day long.
> (Psalm 25:4–6)

Later that day, a friend from church called to check up on me, and we ended up having what, for me, was a fairly therapeutic and insightful conversation. Marlene had always done a great job of being a sounding board for me, and I found that in those discussions with her, my mind would often work its way down a path of discovery. I guess I was essentially thinking through some issue out loud. My friend was concerned for me, which I appreciated, and I found myself explaining to him what had transpired over the previous two-plus years. I assured him that although losing her certainly was not what I wanted, I was beginning to see how God had brought me to this point and had actually prepared me for this precise time.

More than two years earlier, I was presented with that job opportunity that was truly God-directed, as it provided the extra income and benefits we would need to take care of her, even before we knew we would need it. Then months later, nearly losing Marlene in the septic infection health scare was a wake-up call to pay more attention to her needs and to be sure I looked for opportunities to let her know she was loved.

Being only human, I still had some regrets after she passed away, and the suffering she experienced wasn't anything to be desired. But I was thankful for the lessons God taught me at that time as I looked back over those last couple of years and how differently I viewed our relationship, and how I treated her changed. I know from others that have unexpectedly lost a spouse that the regrets and the associated guilt can be a very difficult challenge to deal with, and I was grateful that God's guidance to me saved me from much of that pain.

A year later, the job led me to an even greater opportunity with that company, but one that would require yet another move. After discussing it and prayer, we decided it was worth pursuing. So we put the house up for sale. Meanwhile, the company paid for me to stay in a hotel during the week, and I would commute back home for the weekend. However, we never had any buyers for the house, and after ten months of this, I was wearing out and getting frustrated. I knew something had to change, but I was unsure exactly what.

I felt as though I was in a spiritual wilderness, wandering about, not understanding God's will, and not sensing His direction. Even after soliciting support and prayers from others, including our pastor, there still was no voice, no prompting from the Holy Spirit.

At that point, the manager at our local facility suddenly resigned, which allowed me to transfer back and spend those last few precious months with Marlene at home. Now I am thankful for the house not selling, a house that was now paid off. Looking back at that wilderness time, I understood that, in fact, I was never alone, that God was totally in control and walking me down a path of provision and preparation. I truly believe all of this was God, yet again, being way in front of me, providing for us financially, providing for us emotionally, and preparing me for what was to come.

As I shared this with my friend, it dawned on me that my anxiousness over what would come next was unwarranted. God had a plan, and I needed to have the faith, patience, and insight to discover what that plan was. We ended the conversation with prayer, and I thanked him, again, for his call, although I'm not sure he fully realized just how much a gift from God he was at that time.

The next week, while still sorting through things at the house, I started to work more on finding some type of job that would supplement my income. Living in a small and remote rural town of eight hundred souls, there aren't many job opportunities locally; but after what I had been through, I just couldn't see myself doing any kind of long commute. Even with my years of experience in management, the stress that comes with those types of opportunities wasn't something I was interested in. Besides, I was not convinced there would be many companies interested in hiring someone at my age for that level of responsibility.

I expanded my search and checked for anything that might be available in the next town twenty-two miles away. But nothing seemed to hit me as being what I needed to do, and I never received any response to any of the applications I placed. I prayed to God that He would show me what was next, and a thought kept popping up in my mind: "Be a blessing."

This was something that I had advised Marlene to do when her health forced her into early retirement and, quite honestly, was what was in the back of my mind when I chose to give away either free or at little cost so much of what I was now clearing out of the house.

> Remember this: Whoever sows sparingly will also reap sparingly, and whoever sows generously will also reap generously. Each man should give what he has decided in his heart to give, not reluctantly or under compulsion, for God loves a cheerful giver. And God is able to make all grace abound to you so that in all things at all time, having all that you need, you will abound in every good work. As it is written: "He has scattered abroad his gifts to the poor; his righteousness endures forever." Now he who supplies seed to the sower

and bread for food will also supply and increase your store of seed and will enlarge the harvest of your righteousness. You will be made rich in every way so that you can be generous on every occasion, and through use your generosity will result in thanksgiving to God. (2 Corinthians 9:6–11)

There are so many references in the Bible where God instructs us to be generous, giving people. We are not to be burdened with undue worry over our situation here on Earth, but instead we are to lean heavily on God and His provision for us. Even though I only had a minimal retirement income to start with, I had no debt and few bills, so it made sense for God to be telling me to not worry so much about the money but instead to look to how He could use me.

I live just a block from the campus of our local schools, and it occurred to me that perhaps while I was looking for something more permanent, I could see if they needed a substitute teacher. I had thought that with my mechanical and carpentry skills, they might need help in maintenance as well. So I walked over to the administration office, thinking it was a long shot, but as there simply weren't that many employers in my little town, I couldn't afford to overlook any possibility.

I was met with a smile, and a quick response, to my inquiry: Would I be interested in being a substitute bus driver? I responded cautiously (as I had not considered this as an option) that I would need to think about it.

A couple of days later while watching the morning news, there was a report given on the acute shortage of bus drivers that was creating a national crisis for nearly every school district in the country. I smiled at what I felt was a coincidence, but it did make me think more seriously about the opportunity. Later that morning while I was taking the trash out to the curb, the school superintendent stopped when driving by to ask if I was truly considering driving a bus for the school. I agreed to stop by later to get a better feel for what would be involved, hours, pay, training, and the like. I didn't have a CDL license, so I knew at the very least that would be something I would need.

That night I was struggling to quiet myself to go to sleep, as my mind was racing through so many questions. I asked God if this was what He wanted. Should I pursue this, even though it would likely require a good deal of training for what would be only occasional work? The more I thought about it, the more I prayed and asked for guidance, the more convinced I became that this was not coincidence. This was what God wanted.

So I did agree to become a substitute school bus driver, and when they interviewed me, I told the school that my mission would be not only to get the students back and forth safely but that every child would also get, every morning, a smile and a "Good Morning!" I prayed that I could be a positive adult male influence on these kids.

By the time I began training, the school unexpectedly lost one of their regular route drivers, and they would now need me to take over that route. So now I had a regular work schedule and income. The additional income was exactly enough to meet my financial needs. God's timing is always perfect.

CHAPTER 9

The Holidays

There was still a long road to travel in my journey through grief, but I began to see how God was putting into place what was to become my new life. The house was clearing out and taking shape, I would soon begin training to be a bus driver, and God began to provide much-needed fellowship by putting people into my path.

Marlene and I tended to be introverts. We didn't often go out to dinner or other outside activities, as we were very content to be at home with each other. We were known to quickly enter and leave church, or any gathering for that matter, and this habit was compounded when her health began to deteriorate. She simply couldn't handle large crowds, and walking and standing were both difficult and painful for her. Although at first I kept to this fairly introverted habit, it didn't take me long to realize that even with my comfort zone being alone at home, I needed to be around other people on a regular basis. I remembered a passage in Hebrews:

> And let us consider how we may spur one another on toward love and good deeds, not giving up meeting together, as some are in the habit of doing, but encouraging one another—all the more as you see the Day approaching. (Hebrews 10:24–25)

God was again ahead of me, as while I was learning that I needed to value the importance of this principle, I was invited to help as an usher at church. It was a first, albeit small, step, but it was an important one that began the process of filling my schedule and bringing into my life new friends and support.

Surprisingly, I found myself looking forward to the holidays. Although I knew there would be struggles as I faced the season without Marlene, I think I was happy knowing I could keep busy with the activities brought on by the quick succession of each holiday. I also kept reminding myself of the commitment I made before God: *I choose joy*. I was determined both to relish the fond memories of my life with Marlene and to celebrate God's incredible love for me.

First came Halloween, which ended up being a bit of a disappointment. At that time, New Mexico had some of the strictest COVID regulations in the country which in turn changed so many behaviors and habits. With no grandchildren, Marlene and I both enjoyed seeing and interacting with the kids on Beggars' Night. But for this Halloween, there were only a few who showed up. Undeterred, I shrugged off any negative thoughts and turned my attention to Thanksgiving.

I love to cook and bake, so Thanksgiving always gave me an opportunity to spend a day or so in the kitchen. For me, kitchen time is therapy, both providing quiet time to think through whatever was on my mind and also satisfying my near-constant desire to be creative. For this year, I was committed to doing my best to be thankful for how God had so amazingly been at my side, come tears of sorrow or joy. Other than my younger son, none of the rest of my family lived even remotely close, so it would be just the two of us. Although there were no takers, I contacted the church to let them know that if they came across anyone in my area that needed a place to go for Thanksgiving, my door was open and the table would be full of food.

The menu would be complete with many of the things I so loved about the meal. A turkey breast went in the smoker, and I broke out some of my personal recipes to enjoy. My son helped as well and was also responsible for bringing a bottle of a very fine wine to complete the feast. We spent time sharing memories and talking about his mom, and that evening we were able to reach his brother in Japan via video chat as well. It ended up being a good, meaningful day to give thanks.

My son had already helped me set up the outside lighting display for Christmas, a two-day process. I rearranged things a bit so that my new "Joy" sign would be prominently shown. It was to be an important reminder to me of my commitment to seek the celebration of this season. I guess I also wanted to make a statement for all who knew of my loss, that I was hanging my hat on doing my best to lean on God and face the future in hope and joy.

So with Thanksgiving behind me, I turned on the timers for the outside lights and worked inside to begin the process of getting ready for Christmas by setting up the tree and getting out a few decorations, including the new nutcracker now placed on the hearth. It was good to be so busy for those few days, but once complete, I had to sit down and face the reality that Marlene wasn't there to enjoy the celebration of Christ's birth with me. I was thinking of Jesus's words of comfort to His disciples as He was preparing them for what was to come and for the coming of the Holy Spirit as told in John:

> But the Advocate, the Holy Spirit, whom the Father will send in my name, will teach you all things and will remind you of everything I have said to you. Peace I leave with you; my peace I give you. I do not give to you as the world gives. Do not let your hearts be troubled and do not be afraid. (John 14:26–27)

Peace was certainly something I deeply desired to settle my troubled heart. There were times when I would move forward with plans to enjoy the season only to then feel that old darkness of guilt and loss come over me. It seemed as though every time I would try to celebrate or cherish a happy moment, Satan would once again try to convince me I was being selfish and disrespectful to Marlene, or remind me of just how alone I felt. I prayed that God would give me strength and peace in these attacks and show me the path He had set before me. I knew I needed to do better at quieting myself to clearly hear and understand the Holy Spirit's guidance for me and to experience His strength and comfort.

To me, Thanksgiving and Christmas have always been so closely tied together, and not just on the calendar. I've always felt that Thanksgiving was the perfect way to prepare our minds and hearts to be thankful and to celebrate God's incredible love for us, which He demonstrated so clearly by sending Jesus to us as Emmanuel, "God with us."

One of the things the Holy Spirit also taught me many years ago is that the celebration of Christmas is all about Good Friday and Easter. God gave us His son who in turn would give His life to pay for our sins, and would then defeat death in His resurrection, thereby offering us the promise of an eternity spent praising God and finally seeing Jesus face-to-face. Over the years, it became clear to me just how all of it is so inexorably connected. Those weeks leading up to this Christmas, the season took on a different, deeper meaning. I could see how the Holy Spirit was teaching me to now also celebrate Marlene's release from her earthly pain and struggles. I even found myself envying her at times.

As Christmas approached, I was glad when the church's hospitality team asked me to be one of the ushers for the upcoming

Christmas Eve Eve Service (not a typo as we often do our celebration the second evening before Christmas). Complete with welcoming both familiar faces and guests in our ugly Christmas sweaters, it gave me a time to look outside of myself and to those around me, even if it was just for a relatively short time. Songs, traditional carols, and a meaningful message all helped me to focus on God and His love for us, for me.

Thinking over those last few months since Marlene's death as we ended the evening with singing Silent Night by candlelight, I felt overwhelmed as I recounted in my mind just how much God had been with me every step of the way. But even more importantly, I came to better understand that the promise that Christ's birth points to was, for Marlene, now being fulfilled. This gave me a new appreciation for the celebration of that Christmas. There are no words to express the sense of joy, peace, and happiness that flooded my soul in that moment.

> Silent night, holy night
> Son of God, love's pure light
> Radiant beams from Thy holy face
> With the dawn of redeeming grace
> Jesus Lord, at Thy birth
> Jesus Lord, at Thy birth.

I was now fully ready for Christmas. Although it was a quiet affair with just my son and me, along with a video chat with my older son and daughter-in-law in Japan, it was exactly what I needed. I was thankful that God had granted me a time of peace and rest for those few days, focused on family and God's incredible love for us.

CHAPTER 10

New Year, New Life

It is human nature, I suppose, to view the beginning of any new year as something of a watershed moment. Depending on our circumstances and how we view our lives, for most of us I believe it is either a time of great hope for the promise of a new year, or a time of deepening despair as we see little to be hopeful for.

Although in the past I usually found myself in the former hopeful group, I was facing this particular new year with mixed emotions. After seeing how God had been with me and had been guiding me over those last few months since Marlene's passing, and with the revelations and celebrations of Thanksgiving and Christmas, I was beginning to find hope in anticipation for what God had in store for my future. But I also honestly still felt an emptiness in the part of my heart that missed Marlene, and I was coming to the conclusion I probably always would. Additionally, the control freak part of me experienced some discomfort in not knowing how, exactly, this new year would play out.

I committed myself to finishing my training as a bus driver and completing the last of the tasks around the house I had remaining on my to-do lists. One day shortly after the new year began, I found myself reading in Ephesians, as Paul expressed his prayers and hope for them.

> I pray that out of his glorious riches he may strengthen you with power through his Spirit in your inner being so that Christ may dwell in your hearts through faith. And I pray that you, being rooted and established in love, may have power, together with all the Lord's holy people, to grasp how wide and long and high and deep is the love

of Christ, and to know this love that surpasses
knowledge—that you may be filled to the measure
of all the fullness of God. (Ephesians 3:16–19)

This is what I was praying for myself, that I would fully experience a new hope, a new joyful anticipation. Even more so, I wanted to discover a deeper relationship with God and to understand more completely His love for me. After forty-two years of marriage, my love for Marlene was not something to be simply turned off. I was asking God to help me understand how to deal with this loss and to learn to lean on Him in a new, more significant way. I wanted to "put my whole weight" on Him, but knew I needed His guidance to discover how.

Finally completing my training to be a bus driver and getting my CDL (commercial driver's license), I found great joy and satisfaction driving the students back and forth. Even with a few minor discipline issues, as would be normally expected, the kids have been wonderful to be around, and the staff at the school have been terrific coworkers. It seemed as though there was nothing but confirmation that this was where God wanted me.

As I was approaching age sixty-five, one day I received a notice from Social Security. I had already gotten used to the large volume of mail dealing with my age and an assumed pending retirement. It seemed as though a week didn't go by without notices, ads, and letters from Social Security, Medicare, insurance companies, and senior advocate groups. However, this one took me by surprise.

Social Security was notifying me of a pension I had available from a company I had worked for in the 1980s. That company had long ago been dissolved piece by piece, as it went through several mergers and acquisitions. I had assumed that the pension, although most likely a small one, had long ago been lost through all of this process. But as it turns out, it was still available and had both lump sum and monthly payment components, so I rolled over the bulk payment into my IRA and verified my banking information for the monthly amounts.

Since I had been with that company for only seven years, the dollars given weren't very much, but they did provide yet another piece of my financial future. I thanked God for this unexpected gift.

With strong urging from my younger son, I decided that it was time to perhaps pursue one special purchase, "just for me." We discussed a number of options which included some travel possibilities, but after thought and prayer, I concluded that what I needed was a piano. I was beginning to realize just how much I missed my time at the keyboard and had often felt that my times there were wonderfully therapeutic. Playing the piano is something of a prayer language, with me often becoming lost in thought and listening to the Holy Spirit. Besides, I felt some satisfaction in knowing this would be something Marlene would definitely approve of.

There were several times in those last few years of Marlene's life when she would try to prompt me to spend some money on something she knew I would enjoy. Due to her health, I had given up on the unnecessary extras of life. More than once she would point out a motorcycle, piano, woodworking tool, or other similar item she found for sale in our area. I always refused, telling her I didn't have the time available to justify the expense. While somewhat true, the real reason was I wanted to focus on getting our finances in the best shape possible as I anticipated a retirement that would have our resources stretched as we dealt with her health problems. Never the less, she kept at me and mostly wanted me to get a piano. She knew me well and knew how much having one would mean to me.

So I did some research and settled on a specific digital piano that I felt would hit a sweet spot of providing an accurate acoustic piano experience, but with the easy maintenance and lower cost of a digital piano. However, I soon found out that this particular model was difficult to find, and I had a number of dealers tell me there was a one- to two-year backlog. I kept doing online research and broadening my search further and further from home to find a dealer with this model in stock or soon to arrive, but with no luck.

Desperate, I went to the manufacturer's website to see if I had overlooked any other dealers within a five-hundred-mile radius that carried their products. I was surprised to find that a small music store forty-five miles away was listed. To me it was a long shot, given the size of the store, but was surprised when I called them and was told they had just received one in the last week. I had to smile at the irony when they apologized, as they couldn't deliver it to me for two days. I immediately gave them payment information and arranged the delivery. God truly does work in wonderful ways.

I dug through my things for some of the piano music I still had and was pleasantly surprised to discover that while I was certainly rusty, playing came back to me quickly. The time spent with God while at the keyboard has become an important part of my journey since then.

I discovered God wasn't quite finished with laying out my new life, as opportunities to focus on ministry to others kept coming. Several years earlier, I had looked into helping out with the worship team at my church, but it didn't work out. Now after I had had some time to reinvigorate my keyboard skills, a need for keyboard players came up at church, and I found myself involved with the team, surrounded by wonderful people with a heart and passion for God that I have found truly inspiring. More than that, this put me in the midst of another group of people that God has provided, all of us giving support and prayers for each other.

The timing wasn't right the first time I looked into participating, as my life those next few years were certainly in turmoil. I've learned that part of living in God's will is doing things in His time, not mine.

Later that year, my church partnered with Room 453 Ministry to provide prayer for patients, families, and staff at our local hospital. This involves individuals committing to daily prayer linked to a specific hospital room. In that room, a plaque is mounted to let the patient know someone is praying for them. I was fortunate to be able to be assigned to the same room Marlene had been in, allowing me to anonymously focus on prayer for the patient that may be in that room and the medical staff that are caring for him or her. Because of my own experience, I find myself paying particular attention to the families involved and the stress they may be going through.

I pray for the patient's healing and for peace and strength in what is often the life-and-death struggle that can so often occur in any hospital room. This has been a wonderful way for God to bring me full circle, to now pray for others, as I know so many had prayed for Marlene and me.

Since then, my life has been much like this, with one little "God-incident" after another. My schedule and finances settled into a pattern that has become my new life. It seemed as though with each passing month, I felt more at peace as I learned to lean ever more on God and do my best to better quiet myself to listen to the Holy Spirit. What's more, I was increasingly experiencing a greater sense of God's presence, as though He was wrapping me in arms of strength and love.

CHAPTER 11

Blessed

In the Sermon on the Mount are found the Beatitudes, where Jesus gives a rapid-fire recitation of the blessings we can expect and experience from God. But after having lived this journey through grief over the last two years, I've come to a more meaningful understanding of one in particular.

> Blessed are those who mourn, for they will be comforted. (Matthew 5:4)

In the past and at least at the surface, I had come to understand God's promises to always be true, but I found myself wondering why, with Marlene's death, I struggled to see this promise fulfilled in my life. Even more so, why do so many never find their way out of the darkness of grief?

For myself at least, I had to learn so many lessons, I had to listen more intently to the Holy Spirit, and I had to set aside my own desires and dreams and instead ask God how He wanted to use me. In other words, I had to "put my whole weight" on Him. This is a journey I will be on for the rest of my life, but I can truly say that in spite of the loss and in spite of still missing her, God has already given me great comfort and peace.

However, even more than that, I have, what is to me, an amazing sense of joy for life, and I am truly excited to discover daily what He holds for my future. Luke has a slightly different take on this promise.

> Blessed are you who weep now, for you will laugh. (Luke 6:21b)

The incredible, deep, abundant joy I now have was something I never expected, but then God's promises are always true. Many people, Christ-followers or not, are familiar with the verse of Philippians 20:13, which says, "I can do all this through him who gives me strength." Looking at the full context of this verse, I have come to understand that Paul was not only saying that with the strength that he gains from his faith in Jesus can he deal with any situation, but he was also in fact saying he was, more than just coping.

The Book of Philippians has often been described as the book of joy, rejoicing, and celebration. Based on my own experiences these last few years, I believe Paul was speaking of actually thriving in spite of whatever his circumstances were at any given moment. And that is thriving as God defines it, not as we view it from a worldly perspective. Regardless of where life takes us, there is joy to be found in a fully dependent relationship with God. He gives us what we need, when we need it, if we will only allow ourselves to be open to the possibilities He puts before us. Doing so imparts a sense of joy and celebration.

And this brings me to share a greater understanding of just how important it has been for me to have more than just a very basic exposure to God's Word. I'm not a Bible scholar—in fact, far from it. I've never been very good at memorizing specific verses verbatim, but I am thankful for that heritage of discipline I was raised with, and certainly very thankful for growing up in a Christian home. Over the years, I have managed to read the complete Bible a number of times, and in fact, I've lost count. It has amazed me how many times a passage I've read dozens of times would suddenly leap out at me with a new insight, or speak with a new relevance to whatever situation I was in at the time.

I read through the Old and New Testaments simultaneously as well as the "middle" books (Psalms, Proverbs, Ecclesiastes). By doing so, the Holy Spirit has shown me time and again just how all tied together it is, how wonderful God's promises are, and how patient and loving God is. Now with the new Bible apps available, searching for passages that the Holy Spirit can use to speak to me at any given moment has become extremely easy. My foundation in God's Word, however lacking in my human frailty, has been a tremendous comfort. It has helped me to find both strength and peace as the Holy Spirit has used the Bible to speak to me innumerable times.

I will most likely never experience the trappings of an "abundant" retirement, complete with fun adventures, fine dining, and travel. Living in some exotic location or nice retirement village in a beautiful tropical setting is not in my future. The vehicles I have are in good condition, which is a good thing, as I won't any time soon have the resources to replace them. Even so, I know that for many, these earthly blessings may be the very things God has in store for them, and for them I am happy and thankful. However, for myself, I have found I no longer have a desire for any of these things. I'm content with how God is providing for not only my needs but also for some extra blessings along the way. My joy comes from living in God's will, immersed in His love and enjoying the blessings He has given me.

Over the last year or so, there have been a number of conversations I've had with people who have genuinely wanted to know how I was doing, and more specifically how I had found so much peace and joy. Time and again, I was told of someone they knew who really needed to hear of some of the lessons I've learned. It seems that there are so many who can't find their way through their grief and instead live a life mired in the despair and sadness.

Recently, our church did a series on "Testify," where several people shared in a deep and meaningful way just how God had brought them through some very difficult and dark times. This had an incredible impact on me, as the Holy Spirit overwhelmed me with an understanding that I also needed to testify to God's amazing grace and love, and how He has been walking me down this path of restoration. Paul speaks of this kind of drive to speak and not be silent.

> However, I consider my life worth nothing to me; my only aim is to finish the race and complete the task the Lord Jesus has given me—the task of testifying to the good news of God's grace. (Acts 20:24)

Even though it has only been two years since Marlene's passing, I find myself speaking openly about my experiences. What surprised me, however, was that I felt a strong push from the Holy Spirit to put my experience in writing. I had never attempted such a task and considered myself totally inadequate for what I was being asked to do. I asked God to make sure this direction was very clear to me, to send me a confirmation.

I shared this with one of my new acquaintances in the worship team, asking her to join me in prayer for guidance. She smiled and proceeded to tell me that she has a background in and experience in communications, and had actually helped edit another book project in the past, and that she would be excited to help. I am always amazed to see how God answers prayer and our hearts' desires, and understood this "God-incident" to be the confirmation I was looking for.

So I write this not because I have all the answers, only God does. We all are wired differently and have different life experiences. How God led me may not be how He leads anyone else. As I wrote earlier, we all may have different paths, but we all have the same Guide. My prayer is that somehow through sharing my journey, others will be encouraged to trust God more, to lean on Him more, to quiet their hearts and minds to hear Him more. I have found it is only then that we can find our way through grief to the promise of a life lived in the fullness and joy that only God can provide.

So do I feel blessed? I do, and in amazing ways, and I view this with an overwhelming sense of awe and thankfulness for just how much God loves me. I recently had a conversation with a friend about my experiences, and my eyes got a bit wet as I recited how God was blessing me. Since we had begun by talking about my loss of Marlene, he apparently assumed my tears were for the pain of losing her and said, "You must still really miss her."

I replied, "I do, but these are no longer tears of grief. They're tears of gratitude for where God has brought me."

> Rejoice in the Lord always. I will say it again: Rejoice! Let your gentleness be evident to all. The Lord is near. Do not be anxious about anything, but in every situation, by prayer and petition, with thanksgiving, present your requests to God. And the peace of God, which transcends all understanding, will guard your hearts and your minds in Christ Jesus. (Philippians 4:4–7)

ACKNOWLEDGMENTS

Many thanks to Lauren Healy for your insights and editing assistance. The many hours you spent helping me with this project and your kind support mean more to me than I could ever express.

Thanks to Pastors Ty and Heather Bean, the staff, usher and worship teams, and the many folks at Cowboy Junction Church. Your prayers, kindness, concern, and support have been greatly appreciated. Your willingness to give me opportunities to talk through and share what I was experiencing was such an important part of my ability to go through this journey and helped me learn to express and testify how good God really is.

A special thanks to Room 453 Ministry (https://room453ministry.org/) and Nor-Lea Hospital District for going the extra mile to ensure I was assigned to Marlene's room.

Most importantly, all thanks, praise, honor, and glory to God, for His unfailing love and faithfulness.

ABOUT THE AUTHOR

Phil Winteregg was born and raised near Dayton, Ohio, and currently resides in southeast New Mexico. He and his wife Marlene were married for forty-two years and together raised two sons.

Phil has a background in both music and business and has utilized his talents and training all over the US and abroad. Throughout his life, he has served as a worship leader, music composer and arranger, e-commerce startup creator, business manager, and now, author. Currently a retired businessman, he works part-time as a bus driver and transportation director for his local school district, and he is the alternate municipal judge for his community.

He enjoys time spent at the piano, in the kitchen cooking and baking, working on various remodeling and carpentry projects, and getting his hands dirty as an avid gardener. Phil is a follower of Jesus and an active member of his home church, Cowboy Junction Church, in Hobbs, New Mexico.